Hidden Clover is working to preserve Escudo Island and its inhabitants.
Copies of a Spanish version of *Search for the Hidden Clover: Escudo Island*
have been donated to the children of Ngäbe fisherman who use this land.
Thanks to the Dallas World Aquarium (DWA) for funding the Spanish book printing!

Through your purchase of Hidden Clover books,
we were able to fund signs for the island like the one you see in this book.
Proceeds from book sales continue to fund projects like this.

Thank You.

Also, with help from DWA, the Zoological Society of London (ZSL),
CONAVI, the Minnesota Zoo, Tree Foundation, and other partners,
the Pygmy Sloths of Escudo Island can be saved,
and the island kept beautiful and intact.

Search for a clover, discover the world.

Printed August 2012 in China

Library of Congress Cataloging-in-Publication Data

Heckathorn, Julia
Search for the Hidden Clover: Escudo Island / Julia Heckathorn
Summary: When two children and a kangaroo go searching for a four-leaf clover on Escudo Island, Panama,
they discover wonders of the natural world that they never knew existed.

ISBN: 978-0-9837010-3-3

Library of Congress Control Number: 2012912040

This book is CPSIA compliant

Photo Credit: Pygmy Sloth Photo on Page 16- ©Craig Turner/ZSL

Sign Translation on Page 19 by Lenin Riquelme, and Ngäbe translation on dedication page by Amanda Terry

Ni Ngäbe käi tädre käre kuin bänuäre.

**TO THE NGÄBE PEOPLE,
MAY YOUR LAND STAY FOREVER BEAUTIFUL.**

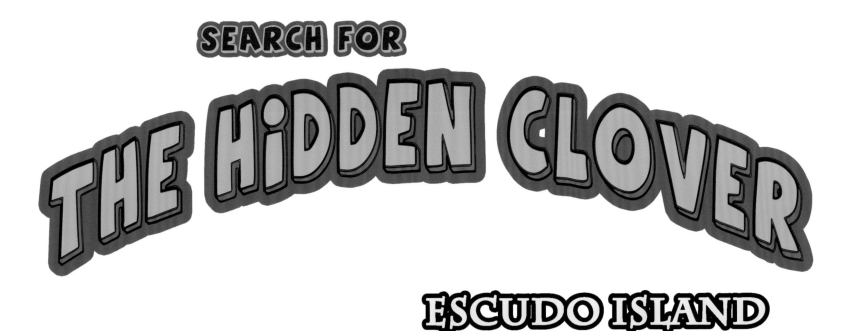

SEARCH FOR THE HIDDEN CLOVER

ESCUDO ISLAND

WRITTEN AND ILLUSTRATED BY JULIA HECKATHORN

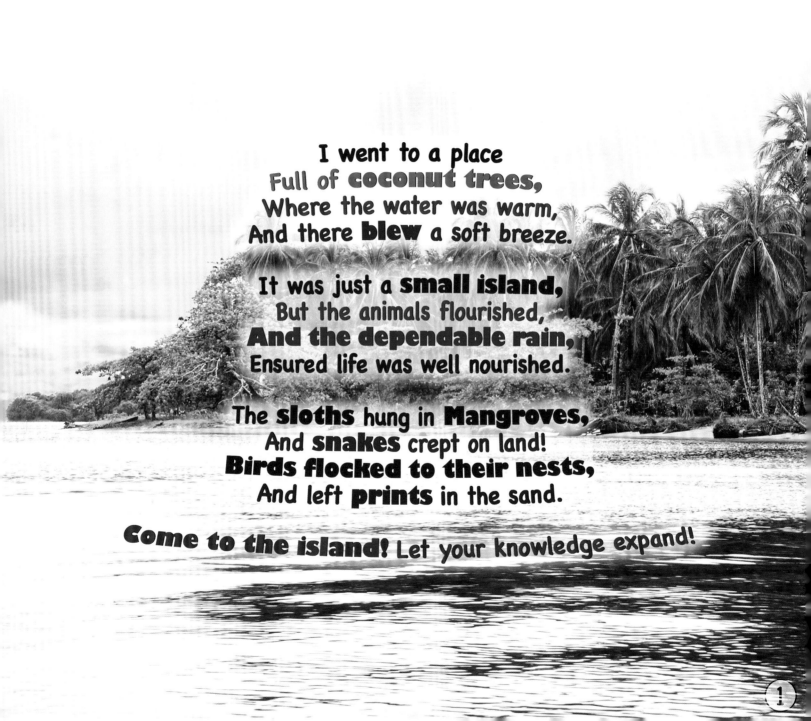

I went to a place
Full of **coconut trees**,
Where the water was warm,
And there **blew** a soft breeze.

It was just a **small island**,
But the animals flourished,
And the dependable rain,
Ensured life was well nourished.

The **sloths** hung in **Mangroves**,
And **snakes** crept on land!
Birds flocked to their nests,
And left **prints** in the sand.

Come to the island! Let your knowledge expand!

Join us in an **ADVENTURE** on **Escudo Island** in Panama, in search of a **4-Leaf Clover**!

Most **4-leaf clovers**
Are quite **HARD TO SPOT**,
But **I know** there's one here,
In this green clover plot!

There's a
4-leaf
clover on this page!
Can you   find it?

Now let's see if we can find a 4-leaf clover on Escudo Island!

③

ESCUDO ISLAND!

"I **see** palm trees and sand!
I **feel** warm breezy air!
It's **Escudo Island**,
We are **finally** there!"

"Who's that **up ahead**?"
Shouted Boomeroo.
"Is that an **ANTEATER**?
He must be visiting too!"

"Who's that **up ahead**?"
Shouted Boomeroo.
"Is that an **ANTEATER**?
He must be visiting too!"

JULIA SAYS

This is a Tamandua, also known as a Lesser Anteater. Tamanduas are smaller than Giant Anteaters, and larger than Silky Anteaters.

⑤

Tamanduas can eat up to 9,000 ants a day!

6 ants have escaped from becoming lunch!
Can you find them?

⑥

We rode to the SHORE, and **jumped** out onto land.

"It's so great to see you,
This is all very **grand!**

You were in **Costa Rica!**
With Daisy! I saw you!
AND NOW you are here,
I can't believe it, WOOHOO!!

I'm NOCHE CUERVO!"

7

"Hello Noche Cuervo,
Our ANTEATER friend!
We came to find **clovers**,
It's the **new** good luck trend!

But they must have **4 leaves**,
Or possibly more!
They are in **clover patches**,
That's what we LOOK for."

8

"I can help you, I'm sure,
But **I need your help** too.
This Island's in **trouble**,
And needs a hand to pull through.

I came to heal Escudo,
But I can't, I'm too small!
I don't have superpowers,
I'm **no hero** at all."

⑨

"You're a **STAR**, Noche Cuervo,
With such a big heart!
You **think** you're too small,
But you're brave and you're smart!

We'll **help** you for sure!
You can **take charge and lead**!
Where should we start?
And what do we need?"

As we walked towards the **mangroves**,
Picking up litter,
We looked down and noticed
A **bright colored** critter!

A little red **Dart Frog**!
Poison and all!
We've seen these before,
But never so small!

⑫

Dart Frogs come in a wide range of colors.
The Dart Frog we met on this island is bright blue and red!

There are 10 Dart Frogs on this page! Do you see them all? 13

"A TRASH PICKING PARTY?
What fantastic fun!
Your work is so helpful,
And can't be undone!"

"Well I'm grateful for help,
And I'm glad we've BEGUN!"

We **waved** and walked on,
When Noche looked up and **sighed**.
We asked what was wrong,
And he softly replied.

"This Island is **home**
To the **most** unique creatures,
Like Pygmy Three-Toed Sloths,
With their tiny sloth features.

They live in these trees,
And are prone to rejection.
Their trees get cut down,
And need our protection."

16

Male sloths have a **SCENT GLAND** on their back to mark their surroundings.

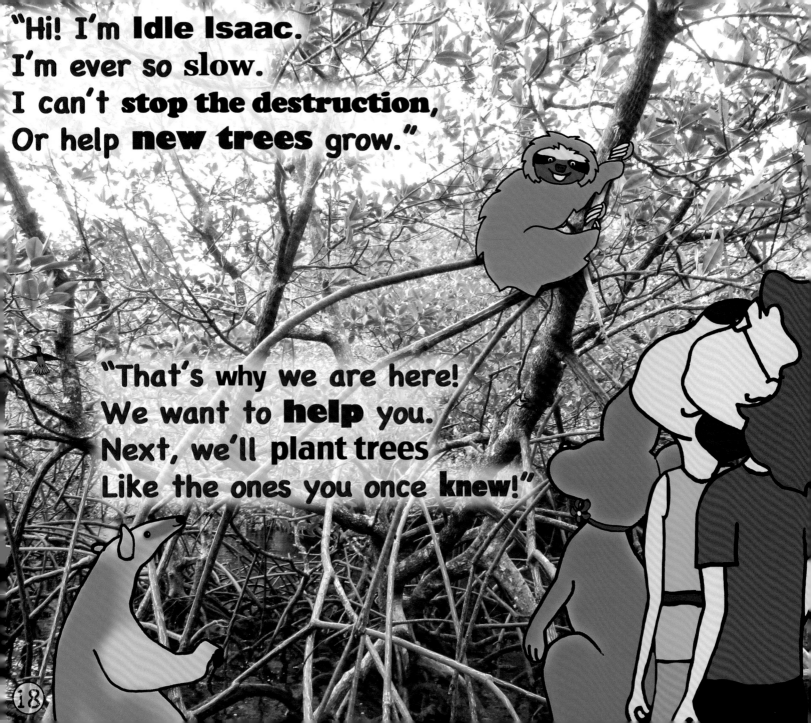

"Hi! I'm **Idle Isaac.**
I'm ever so slow.
I can't **stop the destruction,**
Or help **new trees** grow."

"That's why we are here!
We want to **help** you.
Next, we'll plant trees
Like the ones you once **knew!**"

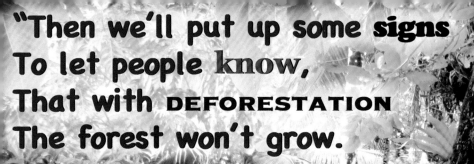

"Then we'll put up some **signs**
To let people know,
That with DEFORESTATION
The forest won't grow.

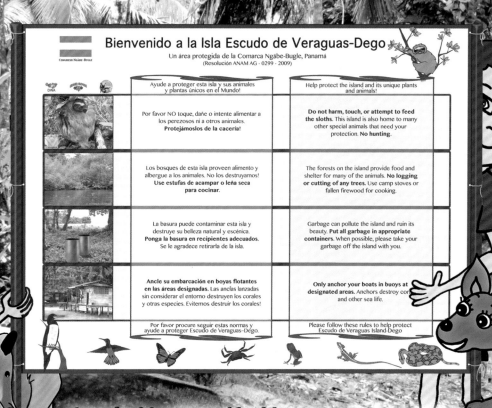

And then all the mangroves
Will flourish once more,
Your **home** will grow large,
Your population will soar!"

7 kinds of animals are using the trees in this picture. Can you find them all?

20

We began **planting trees**,
When we noticed more trash.
And **there** underneath,
Was a small CLOVER stash!

21

We stopped for a moment
To look more intently,
When Boomeroo shouted,
"A 4-leaf clover! Pick gently!"

Do you see the 4-leaf clover?
Now try to find a 4-leaf clover where you live!

22

We were so very happy!
Having just so much FUN,
That we planted in no time,
And in no time, were done!

We had **no** idea
The plans the sloths **made**,
When we walked right into
A SLOW SLOTH PARADE!

"We're ever so **thankful**
For your service and care!
You're **heroes** to us.
You have answered **our** prayer!"

"To Noche we offer,
A CAPE of fine thread.
You're a real superhero,
And will look good in red!

But never let confidence
Go to your head."

YAY CAPTAIN NOCHE!

"What a successful day! Thanks for all of your help! Now it's time for a **termite snack!**

I would share, but I don't think you would find termites very tasty. While i'm snacking, can you TELL ME What you learned today?"

BUT WAIT! THERE'S MORE!

Do you remember all of the animals that you had to find on page 20?
Here are 6 of those animals that are hidden throughout this entire book!

**Look at the numbers below to find out
how many times you have to search for each animal!**

Be sure to include page 20!

4 MONARCH BUTTERFLIES

3 BASILISK LIZARDS

3 MANGROVE CRABS

3 ESCUDO HUMMINGBIRDS

2 BOOBY BIRDS

2 BOA CONSTRICTORS

ABOUT HiDDEN CLOVER

Hidden Clover believes that when people go looking for a small piece of nature,
they discover the fascinating natural world.

Author and illustrator Julia Heckathorn started her company, Hidden Clover,
to deliver a perspective changing experience on nature to children.

Julia started work on her *Search for the Hidden Clover* children's book series in 2009, and
conducts wildlife education at schools, museums, and other organizations. She offers
immersion through books, websites, videos, activities, experiences with nature, and other media.

In pursuit of giving children the truest sense of what these natural areas of the world in her book
are like, Julia visits each region to research and photograph before she writes.

Hidden Clover seeks to serve children, the community, and the world.
The proceeds of her work fund Hidden Clover conservation projects which currently
focus on the preservation of Escudo Island and the critically endangered Pygmy Sloth.

Julia and her husband also strive to regularly serve in ways such as building wells for clean water
in the jungles of Peru, and taking care of exotic animals
for the enrichment of children who learn through the experience of meeting them.

We hope and pray that we are able to inspire others to love and care for nature in a deeper way